✳ Smithsonian

ANIMAL
DISCOVERIES

by TAMRA B. ORR

CAPSTONE PRESS
a capstone imprint

Smithsonian is published by Capstone Press
1710 Roe Crest Drive, North Mankato, Minnesota 56003
www.mycapstone.com

Library of Congress Cataloging-in-Publication Data
Names: Orr, Tamra, author.
Title: Animal discoveries / by Tamra B. Orr.
Description: North Mankato, Minnesota : an imprint of Capstone Press, [2019] |
Series: Smithsonian. Marvelous animals | Audience: Age 7–10.
Identifiers: LCCN 2018005994 (print) | LCCN 2018006891 (ebook) | ISBN
9781543526233 (eBook PDF) | ISBN 9781543526158 (hardcover) | ISBN
9781543526196 (paperback) Subjects: LCSH: Animals—Miscellanea—Juvenile
literature. Classification: LCC QL49 (ebook) | LCC QL49 .O76 2019 (print) |
DDC 591—dc23 LC record available at https://lccn.loc.gov/2018005994

Editorial Credits
Michelle Hasselius, editor, Heidi Thompson, designer;
Svetlana Zhurkin, media researcher; Kris Wilfahrt, production specialist

Our very special thanks to Don E. Wilson, Curator Emeritus, Vertebrate Zoology
at the National Museum of Natural History, for his review. Capstone would also
like to thank Kealy Gordon, Product Development Manager, and the following
at Smithsonian Enterprises: Ellen Nanney, Licensing Manager; Brigid Ferraro,
Vice President, Education and Consumer Products; and Carol LeBlanc, Senior Vice
President, Education and Consumer Products.

Printed and bound in the United States
PA017

Quote Sources
Page 4, "Smithsonian Scientists Discover New Carnivore: The Olinguito." 15
August 2013. Smithsonian Insider. https://insider.si.edu/2013/08/olinguito/

Page 8, "'Fantastic' New Flying Frog Found—Has Flappy Forearms." 14
January 2013. National Geographic. https://news.nationalgeographic.com/
news/2013/01/130114-new-species-flying-frog-vietnam-science-animals-weird/

Page 16, "This Pig-Nosed Rat with Vampire Teeth Will Haunt Your Dreams." 7
October 2015. Live Science. https://www.livescience.com/52417-hog-nosed-rat-
new-species.html

Page 26, "A Whole Load of New Spider Species Have Been Discovered." 15
September 2017. news.com.au. http://www.news.com.au/technology/science/
animals/a-whole-load-of-new-spider-species-have-been-discovered/news-story/
a5600b3da2f1cf08d2fed7c6a35c4412

TABLE OF CONTENTS

Time and Patience. 4

Fantastic Frogs 6

Many Monkeys 10

The Olinguito. 12

The Rinjani Scops Owl. 14

The Hog-Nosed Rat 16

The First Eel 18

The Ghost Ant. 20

The Cambodian Tailorbird 22

Peacock Spiders .24

A Spiny Wasp. 28

    Glossary 30

    Read More 31

    Critical Thinking Questions. 31

    Internet Sites .31

    Index. 32

TIME AND PATIENCE

Look around you. There are a lot of animals living on Earth today. In fact, scientists have identified 1.2 million different types of animals. Do you think we've discovered them all? Not even close. Between 15,000 and 20,000 types of animals are discovered each year. Half of them are insects. Scientists believe up to 7.5 million animals are still waiting to be found.

"... So many of the world's species are not yet known to science. Documenting them is the first step toward understanding the richness and diversity of life on Earth."

—Kristofer Helgen, curator of mammals at the Smithsonian's National Museum of Natural History

Scientists continue to look for new animal species to learn more about the world around us. But discovering these animals takes time and patience. Even after scientists think they have found a new type of animal, there is a lot of work to be done. They must study the animal and talk to other experts to make sure they have something completely new. This can take many years.

FANTASTIC FROGS

THE GLASS FROG

One species of glass frog lives deep in Ecuador's Amazonian forest. Dr. Juan Guayasamin discovered the new frog in 2017. The *Hyalinobatrachium yaku* is less than 1 inch (2.5 centimeters) long. It has dark green spots on its back.

These animals are called glass frogs because the skin over their abdomens is clear. It is possible to see the amphibian's heart, liver, bones, and stomach through its skin.

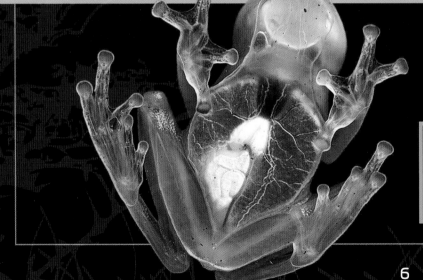

There are more than 150 species of glass frog.

Glass frogs may be small, but they can make a lot of noise. At night they make high-pitched chirps.

THE SMALLEST FROG

U.S. researchers looked through piles of leaf litter to find *Paedophryne amauensis*—the world's smallest vertebrate. In 2010 the researchers were in Papua New Guinea recording frog calls. They heard one call that they couldn't identify. The researchers tracked down the sound and discovered *Paedophryne amauensis*. The frog is only 0.27 inches (0.69 cm) long. It's about the size of a housefly!

HELEN'S FLYING FROG

In 2009 Australian researchers came across a new frog species in Vietnam. Scientist Jodi Rowley named the species Helen's flying frog, after her mother. The frog makes its home in the trees. Its hands and feet are webbed, so it can glide from one tree to another.

"... (it was) one of the most flying frogs of the flying frogs, in that it's got huge hands and feet that are webbed all the way to the toepad."
    —Jodi Rowley

LEGLESS LIZARDS

In 2013 California researchers used pieces of cardboard to catch a new kind of legless lizard. Theodore Papenfuss and James Parham placed thousands of cardboard pieces throughout California. Legless lizards make their homes underground. But sometimes they come to the surface to rest and hunt under dead wood, logs, or cardboard. Papenfuss and Parham discovered four new species of the lizards under their cardboard pieces.

Bakersfield legless lizard

Legless lizards look like snakes, but they can move their eyelids.

MANY MONKEYS

THE CAQUETÁ TITI MONKEY

In 2008 Dr. Thomas Defler discovered a new species of monkey living near the border of Ecuador and Peru. The Caquetá titi monkey has a bushy red beard and is the size of a cat. It even purrs! The Caquetá titi monkey has powerful back legs, which help it leap between trees.

The Caquetá titi monkey is critically endangered. There are less than 250 Caquetá titi monkeys in the wild.

MYANMAR SNUB-NOSED MONKEY

The Myanmar snub-nosed monkey was found in 2010. The animal has large lips and upturned nostrils. When it rains the monkey's nose fills with water, causing it to sneeze. Researchers discovered the monkey by following the sound of it sneezing.

In Myanmar the snub-nosed monkey is called *mey nwoah*. This means "monkey with an upturned face."

THE OLINGUITO

The olinguito was found in the Andes Mountains by Smithsonian scientists in 2013. It was the first carnivore species found in North and South America in 35 years.

The olinguito looks like a cross between a teddy bear and a house cat. At more than 1 foot (0.3 meters) long, it weighs about 2 pounds (0.9 kilograms).

The olinguito has large eyes and thick orange-brown fur. It rarely travels on the ground. Instead, it jumps from tree to tree. The olinguito is active at night, searching for fruit or insects to eat.

Olinguitos have been in museum collections for more than 100 years. But they were mislabeled as olingos. The olingo is a small mammal that lives in trees of the Central and South American rain forests.

olingo

THE RINJANI SCOPS OWL

The rinjani scops is an owl with brown feathers and a white belly. This new owl species was discovered in 2003—once by scientist George Sangster and then a few days later by scientist Ben King. The two scientists had arrived on Lombok separately. Both heard the owl's call. For the next 10 years, Sangster and King worked together to prove the owl was a new species.

The rinjani scops is the first bird found on Lombok. It's named after the second largest volcano in Indonesia, the Gunung Rinjani.

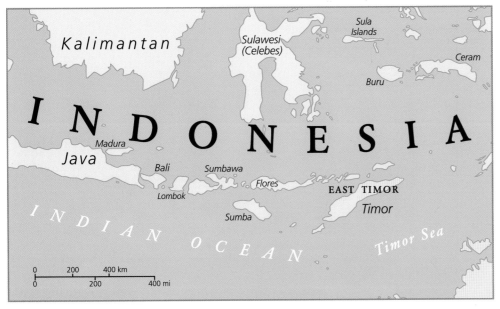

The tiny island of Lombok in Indonesia is east of Bali.

There are 51 known species of scops owls. Most have small ear tufts, small bodies, and brown feathers.

▲
Oriental scops owl

The rinjani scops makes a short whistling call.

THE HOG-NOSED RAT

At first glance the hog-nosed rat looks like a regular rat—until you see its nose. The hog-nosed rat has a long, large nose that turns up. Scientists believe this improves the animal's sense of smell.

The hog-nosed rat was found in 2013 by Jacob Esselstyn, a curator at Louisiana State University's Museum of National Science. Esselstyn found the rat in the forests of Sulawesi Island in Indonesia.

"I have never seen a rat with a nose like that. ... I knew it was a new species. There was never any doubt in my mind."
—Jacob Esselstyn

The hog-nosed rat has sharp, vampire-like teeth.

THE FIRST EEL

The eel species *Protoanguilla palau* may have only been recently discovered, but it has been around for a long time. In 2010 scientist Jiro Sakaue found the eel while he was diving in an underwater cave near the island of Palau. The eel didn't look like other eels alive today. In fact some of its physical features have only been seen on eels that lived more than 100 million years ago.

Scientists studied the eel's DNA. They learned that this animal species dates back 200 million years. This means that this is the oldest known eel species. It has been around 100 million years longer than the oldest eel fossil discovered.

The *Protoanguilla palau* is about 7.9 inches (20 cm) long.

Protoanguilla palau means "first eel from the island of Palau."

THE GHOST ANT

In 2003 Smithsonian scientists discovered a new species of ghost ant. But there is nothing spooky about this tiny insect. Ghost ants are about 0.06 inches (0.15 cm) long. They are found in Caatinga and Cerrado in Brazil.

Ghost ants grow fungus gardens inside their nests. These fungus gardens look like long curtains hanging from the ceiling. They use their gardens for food. Ghost ants are active at night.

Ghost ant nests have tunnels and chambers that are less than 0.04 inches (0.1 cm) wide.

Scientists call the new ghost ant a living fossil. By studying it, scientists may learn how these ants lived millions of years ago.

THE CAMBODIAN TAILORBIRD

Most new bird species are found living in remote places like jungles, rain forests, and other areas away from people. But the Cambodian tailorbird was found in the city of Phnom Penh, the capital of Cambodia. It was first spotted in 2009. The Cambodian tailorbird was officially identified and named in 2013.

"The discovery indicates that new species of birds may still be found in familiar and unexpected locations."
—Simon Mahood, Wildlife Conservation Society

The Cambodian tailorbird is a member of the warbler family. Birds in this group are songbirds that have brightly colored feathers.

prothonotary warbler

The Cambodian tailorbird is one of two bird species that is only found in Cambodia.

PEACOCK SPIDERS

In 2013 two new peacock spider species were discovered in Queensland, Australia. The *Maratus sceletus* has white markings on its body that look like a skeleton. This earned it the nickname Skeletorus. The other spider, *Maratus jactatus*, has red and blue stripes. It's called Sparklemuffin.

Both of these spider species are very small. They measure only 0.1 to 0.3 inches (0.25 to 0.8 cm) long. That's about the size of a pencil eraser.

Skeletorus

Graduate student Madeline Girard discovered the new spider species. She also named them.

Sparklemuffin

Peacock spiders are venomous, but they can't hurt humans. They are so small that their jaws wouldn't puncture our skin.

"They're funny little spiders with these fancy flaps and fancy moves; they are like little birds of paradise. They're so small yet perform and move in such interesting ways. ... They're not scary hairy black things that are dangerous."
—Dr. Jürgen Otto

There are 44 known species of peacock spiders. Males have bright and colorful patterns on their abdomens. To attract a mate, the male peacock spider waves its fuzzy legs and dances. But the male needs to dance well. If the female doesn't like what she sees, she can eat the dancing spider.

People who are afraid of spiders learn more about peacock spiders to overcome their fears.

A SPINY WASP

A new species of wasp has been found—and it has a built-in saw. The adult *Dendrocerus scutellaris* has a sawlike spine that runs down its back. Researchers from Penn State discovered this wasp while studying an insect collection from London's Natural History Museum.

The wasp is less than 0.1 inches (0.25 cm) long. That's about the size of a sesame seed.

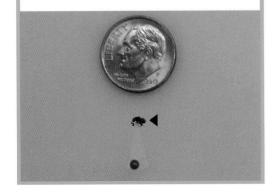

the female *Dendrocerus scutellaris*

the male *Dendrocerus scutellaris*

Scientists believe the wasps lay their eggs inside other insects, called hosts. When the eggs hatch, the new wasps eat their hosts from the inside out. The wasps continue to grow. Then the adult wasps rub their spines to break themselves out of the host.

Scientists believe the wasps live in Costa Rica. But they have never been seen in the wild.

GLOSSARY

abdomen (AB-duh-muhn)—the front part of the body below the chest; the abdomen contains the stomach and intestines

amphibian (am-FI-bee-uhn)—a cold-blooded animal with a backbone; amphibians live in water when young and can live on land as adults

carnivore (KAHR-nuh-vohr)—an animal that eats only meat

curator (kyoo-RAY-tur)—person in charge of a museum collection

endangered (in-DAYN-juhrd)—at risk of dying out

host (HOHST)—a living animal on or in which another animal lives

incisors (in-SIZ-erz)—front cutting teeth found in mammals

mammal (MAM-uhl)—a warm-blooded animal that breathes air and has fur or hair; female mammals feed milk to their young

mate (MATE)—the male or female partner of a pair of animals

puncture (PUHNGK-chur)—a hole or wound made by a sharp object

rain forest (RAYN FOR-ist)—forest typically found in tropical areas with heavy rainfall

species (SPEE-sheez)—a group of plants or animals that share a common ancestor and common characteristics

venomous (VEN-uhm-us)—an animal able to produce a poisonous liquid called venom

vertebrate (VUR-tuh-braht)—an animal with a backbone; mammals, birds, reptiles, amphibians, and fish are vertebrates

webbed (WEBID)—having folded skin or tissue between an animal's toes or fingers

CRITICAL THINKING QUESTIONS

1. There are more than 150 species of glass frog. Name another species of frogs. How is this species different from *Hyalinobatrachium yaku*? How is it similar?

2. Scientists call the ghost ant a living fossil. Name another animal who is considered a living fossil.

2. Why do you think peacock spiders help people overcome their fear of spiders?

READ MORE

Markle, Sandra. *The Search for Olinguito: Discovering a New Species*. Minneapolis: Millbrook Press, 2017.

Rockett, Paul. *30 Million Different Insects in the Rainforest*. The Big Countdown. Chicago: Raintree, 2015.

Spilsbury, Louise A., and Richard Spilsbury. *In the Rainforest*. Science on Patrol. New York: Gareth Stevens Publishing, 2017.

INTERNET SITES

Use FactHound to find Internet sites related to this book.

Visit *www.facthound.com*

Just type in 9781543526158 and go.

Check out projects, games and lots more at **www.capstonekids.com**

INDEX

Australia, 8, 24

Brazil, 20

calls, 7, 14, 15,
colors, 6, 10, 12, 15, 22, 24, 27
Costa Rica, 29

diet, 12, 20, 29

Ecuador, 6, 10
eggs, 29
endangered, 10

feathers, 14, 15, 22

legs, 10
Lombok, 14

noses, 11, 16, 17
nests, 20

Palau, 18, 19
Papua New Guinea, 7
Peru, 10

size, 6, 7, 10, 12, 15, 18, 20, 24, 28
Sulawesi Island, 16

teeth, 17, 19
trees, 8, 10, 12, 13

vertebrates, 7
Vietnam, 8

Some*thing* Might Happen

HELEN LESTER

Illustrated by LYNN MUNSINGER

Houghton Mifflin Company Boston 2003

Walter Lorraine Books

To my son Robin, who chose to be there when something happened. —H.L.

Walter Lorraine (wn) Books

Text copyright © 2003 by Helen Lester
Illustrations copyright © 2003 by Lynn Munsinger

www.houghtonmifflinbooks.com

Library of Congress Cataloging-in-Publication Data

Lester, Helen.
   Something might happen / Helen Lester ; illustrations by Lynn Munsinger.
      p. cm.
   Summary: Twitchly Fidget the lemur worries about almost everything until
his Aunt Bridget Fidget pays him a visit and shows him another way to live.
   ISBN 0-618-25406-4
   [1. Worry—Fiction. 2. Fear—Fiction. 3. Lemurs—Fiction. 4. Aunts—Fiction.]
I. Munsinger, Lynn, ill. II. Title.
   PZ7.L56285So 2003
   [E]—dc21
                                                        2002156428

Printed in the United States of America
WOZ 10 9 8 7 6 5 4 3 2 1

Twitchly Fidget trembled all over.
No, nothing had happened to him.
But it might.

Twitchly was afraid of almost everything.
His bottle of shampoo sat unopened on the shelf.

What if he got all bubbly, and the shampoo wouldn't rinse off, and birds would be attracted to his head, thinking he was a bubblebath, and they'd stay there for weeks?

He wouldn't eat his cereal because the crunchy noises might
startle him, causing him to jump and hit his head on the lamp.

He found his sneakers especially scary. Suppose he put
them on the wrong feet and he had to walk cross-legged for
the rest of his life?

Twitchly lived in a leafy little hut he had carefully designed. No windows or door. Something might want to get in. And no roof. After all, a roof could cave in.

Twitchly put a hat on his doll so its big, spooky eyes wouldn't frighten him.

And there he sat in his dreary little
hut, waiting for something to happen.

Knock knock.

Twitchly twitched.
Somebody was at his nondoor.

"Twitchly," called his fellow lemurs,
"you must come! There's going
to be a parade today, with drums and
trombones and everything!"

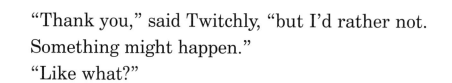

"Thank you," said Twitchly, "but I'd rather not.
Something might happen."
"Like what?"

"Like I might get bopped with a drumstick or
sucked up in a trombone."
So the lemurs left until another day.

Knock knock.
Twitchly flinched.
"Twitchly," called his fellow lemurs,
"you must come! There's going to be a
big marshmallow roast. All you can eat!"

"Thank you," said Twitchly, "but I'd rather not.
Something might happen."
"Such as?"

"Such as, what
if a marshmallow
got stuck on my shirt
and I backed into
another lemur with a
marshmallow stuck on his
pants and he backed into another
lemur with a marshmallow stuck on her hair bow . . ."
Twitchly shivered as his voice trailed off.
So the lemurs left until another day.

Knock knock.
Twitchly shuddered.
"Twitchly," called his fellow lemurs,
"you simply must come! There's
going to be a huge Fourth of
February party, with funny hats,
confetti, and even balloons!"

GO
AWAY

NO ONE
LIVES
HERE

Twitchly

"Thank you," said Twitchly, "but I'd rather not.
Something might happen."
"WHAT thing?"

"Well, my funny hat might fall over my eyes and I'd trip
into a pile of confetti and get so buried no one would
ever find me. And baboons? Even BABOONS?"
So the lemurs left.

Then one day something DID happen.
Twitchly Fidget's Aunt Bridget Fidget dropped in
for a vidgit. A visit.

And she was none too pleased as she rearranged her clothes. "You certainly don't make it easy, having visitors plunge through your nonroof," she snapped.

"And just look at you. Mussy hair, skinny as a snake, and no shoes. You need a fixin'."

Twitchly twitched. A fixin'.

Aunt Bridget Fidget squirted a large blob of shampoo onto
Twitchly's head, and in no time had worked him into a lather. Then
she hosed him down and off came the bubbles, just like that.

Twitchly couldn't believe it. Nothing happened.

"Now open wide."

Aunt Bridget Fidget came at Twitchly with a loaded spoon, and as he opened his mouth to scream, she shoveled in a large serving of cereal.

Stuck with a mouthful,
Twitchly chewed.

Crunch. Crunch. Crunch.

Oddly, he was so taken
with the delicious flavor, the
crunching sound didn't bother him.
And nothing happened.

Aunt Bridget Fidget went on. "You know, young man, what I've always said about going barefoot. Gives you dusty feet. Now on with those sneakers."

Twitchly trembled.
Which was the right?
Which was the left?

Slowly he put the left shoe on his right foot
and the right shoe on his left foot.

Then, knees knocking,
he stood up —
and he WALKED.

Almost normally.

And nothing happened.

27

"And take that silly hat
off your doll!"

Twitchly did.
Not so scary after all.
Aunt Bridget Fidget eyed Twitchly, surveying her handiwork.
"That's an improvement. A definite improvement."
Satisfied, she turned to leave.

But wait. There was a problem.
"How in the leafy green world
do you expect me to get out
of here? Fly?"

Twitchly, feeling fluffy, full, and fashionable
in his sneakers, had the answer.

With nimble fingers he dug out a window.
Then another. And finally a door.

He planted a big smooch on Aunt Bridget Fidget's furry
cheek and waved goodbye.
Then he set out on his own to look for wonderful parades.
For marshmallow roasts.
And he couldn't wait until the next Fourth of February.